SARAH JAKES

COLLIDING
~ *with* ~
DESTINY

A 30-DAY JOURNEY
THROUGH THE BOOK OF RUTH

BETHANY HOUSE PUBLISHERS

a division of Baker Publishing Group
Minneapolis, Minnesota

© 2013 by Sarah D. Jakes, LLC

Published by Bethany House Publishers
11400 Hampshire Avenue South
Bloomington, Minnesota 55438
www.bethanyhouse.com

Bethany House Publishers is a division of
Baker Publishing Group, Grand Rapids, Michigan

Printed in the United States of America

ISBN 978-0-7642-1210-9

Cover and interior design by Lookout Design, Inc.
Cover photograph: Nick Swanson

Author is represented by Dupree/Miller & Associates

To all my friends on a journey
who want to believe
there's joy after their pain.

CONTENTS

INTRODUCTION

*N*ow that we're adults, my brother and I have created this new tradition. Whenever we stay at my parents' home, we take the opportunity to spend some quality time together. He loves being an uncle to my kids, and I love for them to get to know him. So after the kids have finished their homework, had supper, and taken their baths, we all settle in to relax together. Whether it's watching something on television, spending time talking about each other's day, dancing around to music, or play fighting, we always have fun.

Sometimes we even turn our hanging out into a team sport! Yes, the girls versus the boys, sibling teams versus sibling teams, or school versus school. Everything except for the play fights—that comes down to Malachi, my son, and Dexter, my brother. I just commentate or instigate, proving an important role in the morale of the fight.

One evening recently, we were trying to teach Malachi the art of boxing. Dexter and I would emulate the proper stance, bounce, and posture. But we also stressed the most important factors: heart and attitude. Turning the family room into a makeshift boxing ring, we all burst into laughter as my six-foot-four little brother and five-foot-three son playfully squared off. Imitating Floyd Mayweather and Muhammad Ali, they both turned it all the way on!

After they engaged in this lighthearted contest, I again tried to show Malachi a boxer's stance. At ten years old, he had never seen an actual fight, so he had no clue what to do.

"Watch this," I said and gave my best Laila Ali impression. *Bounce, bounce. Bob, weave. Uppercut. Jab, jab. Bounce. Weave.* My son, timid in nature, looked up at me with wide eyes.

"But, Mom, I can't even reach his face!" he explained.

I looked at him and smiled. But before I opened my mouth to reply, I heard, "I CAN REACH HIS FACE, MAMA!"

I looked down at my three-year-old, three-foot-high daughter, Makenzie. In perfect Laila Ali stance, down to the rhythm of her bounce, Makenzie was prepared to take on Dex. She had been watching us the whole time. Never recognizing their differences in size, she was ready to face the challenge.

Makenzie had no concept of how much smaller she was in comparison to her competition. All she knew was that she had the heart to fight the battle. It didn't occur to her to be intimidated by someone bigger.

What if we dared to believe with the heart of a child?

Somewhere along the path of life, we start to size up the competition. We start to look at how big the challenge before us is and get discouraged. Little by little, the punches of life begin to bruise our hope. We stop fighting as hard as we once did because we don't believe we can win anymore. We don't block very well because we're expecting the knockout that will end it all. We stop living, out of fear.

Fear is the most shameful ghost of them all. Painful memories of past fights convince us that some things are not worth the risk of fighting at all. We allow our past to dictate our every move. We stand in place and wait for life to hit us again.

Certainly we're taught to always keep the faith. But when life's blows rock us to our core, it's hard to remember that our pain has a purpose. When the aches of what happened, what should have happened, and what could have happened haunt our every decision, keeping the faith can be a challenge.

If disappointments have kept you from being your true self, then this book is for you. My friend, please allow me to share with you the story of Ruth—*all of her story*, not just the happy ending. We often hear of Ruth having her Boaz, but we rarely discuss the collisions she faced on the road to her destiny. While it's imperative that we remember her legacy, we can only give it value if we see the price she paid for it.

Could it be that if you dare to live again, your story doesn't have to be associated with what broke you? That by doing whatever it takes to survive, you will sow seeds of redemption into your future?

Ruth's story begins with her being an outcast. Shunned in her homeland of Moab because she left the religion of the land and embraced her husband's beliefs, Ruth remained committed to her new husband and new God. And then again, when she returned to her mother-in-law's hometown, Bethlehem, she was shunned for being a foreigner from a pagan land. She carried the burdens of both who she was and who she used to be.

When Ruth worshiped with her husband's family in her

hometown, there was a religious differentiation that caused her to be an outcast. She no longer bowed to their idols or prayed to their false gods. In Bethlehem, she was talked about because of her mystery. It was what people didn't know about her that intrigued them the most. She seemed like them, but on the inside she was not the same.

Ruth knew that sometimes it's our silent heartaches, the ones that bring tears to our eyes and make us want to drown the pain, that often separate us from others. But she also knew the faithfulness of her Lord, the ways He transformed her pain into His perfection. The trials that Ruth endured on the way to her collision with destiny offer hope to each of us. Whether what has broken you can be seen by the world or is a silent burden you whisper in your pillowcase at night, God can still use your struggle to propel you to your destiny!

Ruth's story has inspired me to share with you a thirty-day devotional to help aid you on your journey of colliding with divine destiny. It is my prayer that this devotional will release clues from God that lead you back to Him like never before. It is my hope that your spirit will be refreshed, uplifted, and upheld as you move forward to the treasure that awaits you.

While studying the book of Ruth, I was reminded that God can restore life's most damaging collisions. In my time with Ruth, I learned that survival is so much more than a perky smile and dozens of friends. It's more than pretending to have it all together on the outside. Survival just means you do what you can with what you have left. And trust that God will do the rest.

Whether your heart has been broken because love had a devastating ending for you or your body has been ravaged by a painful disease, this book is for you. Or maybe you have a past you feel you can't escape. Maybe you're trying to reinvent yourself after life has dealt you its hardest blow. Maybe each day is an excruciating battle with depression. Maybe you're surrounded by other people while suffering the inner loneliness of not belonging. No matter what it is, you *will* have something in common with Ruth.

Imagine yourself being free. Bright-eyed, three-year-old Makenzie/Laila Ali free. Imagine looking at the size of life's battles without fear. What if you trust me and begin to believe that the barrier that blocked you from your destiny can be the platform God uses to propel you into your destiny? No longer will you be ruled by an imperfect past, difficult present, or grim future.

Think you'll have to be superwoman to do it? Spend thousands of dollars and dozens of years to get there? Learn eight languages to understand it? You're wrong!

I can show you one woman who faced many trials. Some because of the decisions she made and others because she was a victim of the choices of others. Still, she found a way to continue on her journey.

Survival can be a tricky road. It can be difficult to remember why we must press forward. Life can numb us so much we no longer want to remember who we are. If you're reading this book, it's because you want to remember. You want to try and to survive again.

You want to believe that there is life after the memories . . . the pain . . . the rumors . . . and the lies. You want to get through today trusting that tomorrow will be better. You don't know how you'll keep going, only that you can't stop now. If these ring true, then you are on the same journey of survival that became the red carpet for Ruth's coming-out party.

Can you feel it? God is already beginning to restore you. With His help, please allow me to guide you through the story of Ruth so that you, too, can experience your collision with destiny.

Sarah Jakes

P.S. One day I'll tell you about my collision with destiny story, too! Watch for *Lost and Found* in spring 2014!

LIFE DOESN'T ALWAYS GO AS PLANNED

Just because you make a change for the better doesn't mean you escape trouble. It only means your trouble has a promise.

In the days when the judges ruled, there was a famine in the land. So a man from Bethlehem in Judah, together with his wife and two sons, went to live for a while in the country of Moab. The man's name was Elimelek, his wife's name was Naomi, and the names of his two sons were Mahlon and Kilion. They were Ephrathites from Bethlehem, Judah. And they went to Moab and lived there.

Now Elimelek, Naomi's husband, died, and she was left with her two sons. They married Moabite women, one named Orpah and the other Ruth. After they had lived there about ten years, both Mahlon and Kilion also died, and Naomi was left without her two sons and her husband.

RUTH 1:1–5

*W*e make idols out of so many things in our lives. Whether we're just getting by or finally getting ahead, we discover that cars, clothes, careers, relationships, and money all have a way of clouding our vision, pulling our focus away from God. Eventually, we learn that we cannot serve two masters. We must choose and prioritize what's most important to us. We have to draw the line between enjoying things and worshiping things.

It's usually not until we encounter trouble that we reassess what we consider valuable and learn that things are just that—things. Whether it's divorce, loss of income, death of a loved one, or some other life-changing moment, we finally find ourselves at a crossroad. What do we do when life doesn't go as planned? Will we become bitter? Or will we seek God in the midst of our loss and become better?

Ruth, a Moabite woman, grew up practicing the religion of her land. Although she was raised to worship many gods, there was only One who could prepare her for her destiny. When Ruth married Mahlon, she didn't marry just him. She married his God. Finding fulfillment in her marriage and her new faith, Ruth appeared to be living her dream. Ten years later her dream turned into a nightmare.

What do you do when life doesn't go as planned? You've finally sown all the right seeds, and yet all you reap in return is heartache. We hardly ever question God when things go like we want. But when we face trouble, we want answers. Where is God in the midst of our life's most painful disappointment?

It's so easy to see Him when things are going our way. But are you willing to do the work it takes to discover Him in the midst of your disasters? He never promised there wouldn't be trials. He never promised we wouldn't have to wipe away some tears along the way.

What He has promised us is that we are not tested with any obstacle we can't overcome. And we will never have to face the harsh winds of life alone. God is there with us and has equipped us—long before He trusted us with the struggle.

When we decide to make Him ruler of our lives, we do so knowing that each day may not be easy, but each will serve a purpose. Just as Ruth could not anticipate that the death of her husband would be the beginning of her new life, we also lose sight of the fact that our troubles are only temporary. Even after having and losing it all, we must remember that whatever—or whoever—we lost, we have not lost God.

Sometimes He removes all the distractions from our lives so that we can focus solely on Him. Do not give up when life doesn't go as planned. Instead, remember that all things work together for our good when we live a Christ-led life. The things that cause us the most pain are usually the roots that develop our true purpose. So weep, feel the pain, find a release for your anger, and sort through all the grief, but don't give up on God. He's there in the midst of it all.

JOURNAL

When you were younger, what was the plan you had for your life?

What has gotten in the way of this plan being realized?

How has the pain of losing your plan affected you?

How have your views on God changed as a result of the unexpected shift?

PRAYER

God, I admit I'm lost, hurt, and confused. I've remained silent for too long, and now it's time to give my pain a voice. It's time for me to catch my breath and face what's ahead. I know I must accept that I'm broken before I can be healed. I need You, Lord. And like Ruth, I'm willing to follow You to my divine destiny. Amen.

UNMASKING THE LONE RANGER

We often try to protect people from our trouble, but if someone
is willing to walk through it with you, don't turn them away.

Then [Naomi] arose with her daughters-in-law that she might return from the land of Moab, for she had heard in the land of Moab that the Lord had visited His people in giving them food. So she departed from the place where she was, and her two daughters-in-law with her; and they went on the way to return to the land of Judah. And Naomi said to her two daughters-in-law, "Go, return each of you to her mother's house. May the Lord deal kindly with you as you have dealt with the dead and with me. May the Lord grant that you may find rest, each in the house of her husband." Then she kissed them, and they lifted up their voices and wept. And they said to her, "No, but we will surely return with you to your people." But Naomi said, "Return, my daughters. Why should you go with me? Have I yet sons in my womb, that they may be your husbands? Return, my daughters! Go, for I am too old to have a husband. If I said I have hope, if I should even have a husband tonight and also bear sons, would you therefore wait until they were grown? Would you therefore refrain from marrying? No, my daughters; for it is harder for me than for you, for the hand of the Lord has gone forth against me."

And they lifted up their voices and wept again; and Orpah kissed her mother-in-law, but Ruth clung to her.

Then she said, "Behold, your sister-in-law has gone back to her people and her gods; return after your sister-in-law."

RUTH 1:6-15 NASB

good friend of mine went through a cancer scare. She called to let me know that she'd had some tests and the doctor wanted her to come in so they could discuss the results. I was due to go out of town on the day of her appointment, but I canceled my trip and told her I'd be there. She insisted that she would be fine going alone and found a thousand different ways to tell me canceling my trip was senseless. After several unsuccessful attempts to get me to change my mind, she finally gave in and allowed me to join her.

For me, being there wasn't something I did out of friendly obligation. I wanted to be there, because I needed her to remember that regardless of what the results were, she was not alone. I needed her to remember something we all need to hear when we're soaked by the storm.

Fear cannot isolate you if you allow love to surround you.

When your life has been shattered into pieces, it's hard to believe anyone would want to help you clean up the mess left behind. It's easier to push people away than to admit you're scared. It's easier to suffer in silence.

Naomi had buried her husband and, ten years later, lost both of her sons. Realizing their wives, Orpah and Ruth, were still young women, Naomi encouraged them to go their separate ways. She realized that their only connection to her died when she buried her sons.

Uncertain of what lay ahead of her, she pleaded with them to go back to their former lives.

While Orpah heeded the older woman's counsel, Ruth refused to hear any of it. She was not going back. She was going forward—with Naomi.

How many times have we tried to protect people from going through trials with us? We pretend we're okay so others don't see just how broken we are. When we need people the most, we push them away, afraid they'll see our truth. Or worse . . . see our truth and then leave us.

It's hard to believe someone would volunteer to go through the trouble you can't bear to face yourself. As difficult as it may be to trust again, you have to give people a chance to be there for you the way you've been there for them. When we are fragile, it's easier to be carried by love than to be left alone in our grief. Solitude is dangerous when grief is inescapable. Yes, you are capable of winning without the support of other people. With God's help, you have the endurance and the strength to make it, even if you don't have anyone on your team. But why do it alone if you don't have to?

Over two thousand years ago, a Man was bruised for our iniquities and wounded for our transgressions. But even He needed help to carry the cross God had given Him. It doesn't change the trajectory of your destiny or the power of your testimony when someone eases the burden of your cross.

JOURNAL

When was the last time you made the decision to stand with someone instead of leaving in hard times?

Why did you make that decision?

How did this person respond? Were they grateful for your loyalty?

How do you acknowledge God in hard times? Do you view Him as your judge or lawyer?

PRAYER

God, I know You will never leave me or forsake me. Please give me the wisdom to identify Your hand in every area of my life. Help me to recognize the people You bring across my path who can help me navigate life's storms. Reveal to me those special people with whom I can trust the pieces of my heart. Amen.

KEEP THE FAITH

When events in life get harder,
that's when our faith must run deeper.

But Ruth replied, "Don't ask me to leave you and turn back. Wherever you go, I will go; wherever you live, I will live. Your people will be my people, and your God will be my God. Wherever you die, I will die, and there I will be buried. May the Lord punish me severely if I allow anything but death to separate us!" When Naomi saw that Ruth was determined to go with her, she said nothing more.

RUTH 1:16–18 NLT

*E*very New Year I start off with one resolution: lose weight. With renewed enthusiasm, I am dedicated to changing my eating habits, getting fit, and exercising consistently. Of course, I have to start on the second because we always have a big New Year's Day feast. Well, actually, I start on the fifth because my brother's birthday is on the fourth, and we usually have a special family dinner. Now that I think about it, it's more like a few weeks later. I like to host watch parties for all the big award shows, and no one wants to eat celery and carrots. And somehow I always manage to find a hundred more reasons not to start. Before I know it, it's November, and I'm ten pounds heavier than I was when I made my resolution!

Last year was different, though. I went to the gym religiously. I learned which foods I could eat at our family feasts and remain healthy. The extra weight was literally falling off. Then a strange thing happened.

Around mid-February, I was no longer losing weight as rapidly. I'd drop a pound or two every few weeks, but not the number of pounds I'd become accustomed to. By March, I was discouraged. After working out with my trainer, I finally voiced my complaint. The trainer smiled at me as if he'd heard this same complaint before. He explained that when you work out frequently, your body starts gaining muscle—so you continue to lose inches, but not necessarily weight. So even though I hadn't wavered in my commitment, and I knew changes were happening, I wasn't seeing the results in the way I expected.

As Ruth looked into the eyes of her mother-in-law, surely she thought about the commitment she had made to her husband—and her husband's God. Although it appeared that life wasn't working in her favor, something inside of her refused to go back to the way things had been. Naomi begged Ruth to turn around and go back where she came from. But Ruth refused to give up.

From her limited perspective, it didn't look like her new faith was working. Her dedication didn't appear to be paying off. Little did she know that God, in His infinite wisdom, was working it out in ways she couldn't even imagine, let alone see yet. All she knew was that she couldn't give up on her new faith. She couldn't just abandon her mother-in-law and pretend that she didn't care.

Ruth was losing inches, but carrying the same weight.

Don't let discouragement block your blessing. Just because it doesn't look like God is working for you doesn't mean your commitment isn't paying off. You don't know when or where you'll reap your harvest, but you can trust that God sees your seeds. Even if you don't see it now, you're moving toward your destiny.

JOURNAL

What are you hoping God will change for the better in your life?

What have you remained committed to even though the results haven't been evident? Why?

What has made you give up in the past? What will make you stay faithful now?

PRAYER

Lord, please help me to remember that it takes time to grow and change. Remind me that there is time between when a seed is planted and when the fruit is produced. Give me patience and stamina. Help me not to grow weary and become shortsighted. Grant me Your strength so that I may persevere through the process. Amen.

DON'T LET LIFE
CHANGE YOUR NAME

"It ain't what they call you, it's what you answer to."

—attributed to W. C. Fields

So the two women went on until they came to Bethlehem.
When they arrived in Bethlehem, the whole town was stirred
because of them, and the women exclaimed, "Can this be
Naomi?"

"Don't call me Naomi," she told them. "Call me Mara,
because the Almighty has made my life very bitter."

RUTH 1:19–20

*T*he first thing you learn about a person is his or her name. It is the way we introduce ourselves to the world. When we agree to terms on something, such as a contract or loan, we sign our name. Our name is how we want to be remembered. Our name represents who we are and who we're called to be.

After burying her husband and two sons in a foreign land, Naomi was bitter. So bitter that she decided to change her name to Mara, another way of saying the same thing. She mourned through an endless night and couldn't imagine ever feeling joy again. She didn't feel like the person she used to be, so she figured she might as well become what she felt. Her grief had consumed all that was inside her, right down to the essence of her identity.

Our losses and mistakes often try to redefine us. *Liar, cheater, dummy, fool, adulterer*—life gives us countless titles. At some point we've all done or experienced something we're not proud of. Whether deliberately or inadvertently, we've all made decisions that led to devastation. Like someone suffering amnesia, in the midst of our pain we may face an identity crisis. Will we remember who we've always been, or will this hurt be what now defines us?

When the memories of what should have been invade your soul and shake your core, whatever you do, don't let it change your name. You don't want the agony of your pain to be the aroma that lingers behind when you exit a room. You don't want to reward misery by allowing it to be the center of your life. We have to be careful about the feelings we allow on the center stage of our hearts. For "out of the abundance of the heart the mouth speaks" (Matthew 12:34 NKJV).

In our pain, how then do we reconcile our true feelings with our faith? Sure, we know what we're supposed to say and think. We know that vengeance belongs to the Lord and that others will reap what they sow. We know the "right answers" and how we *should* be feeling. When you've cried for months and months, though, it gets difficult to believe that weeping will only endure for a night.

Even when we feel labeled by life's losses, we must never let the pain push us into being someone we're not—someone hopeless, angry, bitter, resentful. It doesn't mean you can't feel those moments. We all have times when we're overwhelmed with emotion, but we have to find a way out.

Decide what you want your name, your legacy, to be and declare it over your life. Do you want to be remembered as hostile, vicious, or spiteful? Or do you want the world to remember how you survived and learned to live again?

Naomi was stricken with grief. She wanted to face the pain alone, but God allowed Ruth to be a part of her journey. Ruth, someone who knew her in better days, could remind Naomi who she once was. Don't miss the moments when God sends you a reminder of who you were meant to be. Joy can only come in the morning if you remember to open the curtains and let in the morning light.

JOURNAL

How do you define yourself? What words would you use to describe who you really are?

How do you want to be remembered?

When have you allowed your pain to make you forget your destiny?

How would the healed you be different from the hurt you?

PRAYER

If you, like Naomi, have lost your purpose, remember that God has one greater in store for you. As you go to God in prayer, ask Him to remind you. Pray, "God, help me to see myself the way You see me. Open my eyes so that I can see beyond this broken place. I want to discover my potential. I want to believe there is life after this. Remind me of the truth of Your Word, "that all things work together for good to those who love God, to those who are the called according to His purpose" (Romans 8:28 NKJV). When I feel I've lost my purpose, help me to remember that You have one greater in store for me. Amen.

STICK WITH
WHAT YOU KNOW

*When life leaves you empty, you must return
to the foundation of what you know for sure.*

"I went out full, and the Lord has brought me home again
empty. Why do you call me Naomi, since the Lord has testi-
fied against me, and the Almighty has afflicted me?"

So Naomi returned, and Ruth the Moabitess her daughter-
in-law with her, who returned from the country of Moab. Now
they came to Bethlehem at the beginning of barley harvest.

RUTH 1:21-22 NKJV

*L*ast Christmas, my daughter wanted a Dora the Explorer bicycle. After driving across town, checking several stores, waiting in line, and finally getting the bicycle, I was elated. I couldn't wait to see her face when she saw the bike for the first time. On Christmas Eve, after wrapping the last of the kids' gifts and placing them under the tree, I remembered the bike.

Tired and eager to relax, I quickly started putting it together. I didn't bother with the instructions. The pieces just looked like they would fit. After all, it was a Dora bike; how hard could it be?

As it turned out, it was *much* harder than it looked. After several attempts, I took everything apart again, read the instructions, and finally discovered the way things were supposed to go all along. I laughed at myself and realized that so often this is the way things go in life. We jump in and think we know how all the pieces fit, only to learn the hard way that our way is not the right way. We have to go back to the certainty of our instructions.

Ten years before her crisis, Naomi found herself looking at all the pieces of her life, thinking she knew exactly how things would turn out. She did everything she knew to do, everything that made perfect sense. But in the wake of such devastating loss, life began whispering, letting her know that God's plan was better than her own.

We have all had these moments, these devastating blows that

leave us lost. In our confusion, we seek something to numb our pain. We seek distractions to keep us from remembering the disappointment of our plans falling apart. Instead of getting frustrated and throwing the scattered pieces of my daughter's bike in the trash, I had to take a deep breath and start over. Naomi had to return, humbled and grief-stricken, back to the place where she had started.

Sometimes the only way to move forward is to go back to what we know and start again. Naomi didn't just go home so that she could start over. After losing her children and husband, she had also lost the significant roles in which many women find their purpose and identity. Now more than ever, she needed to return to the people who could help her remember who she really was.

How many times have we had to start over? New career. Foreclosed home. Divorce. School. Life has a way of giving us the option of humbling ourselves or numbing ourselves. Do we try to move on as if nothing has happened, or do we dare admit that we must start again? Often our pride prevents us from admitting that life has dealt us a blow. We pretend that we have it all together. We invent stories that suggest we aren't as broken as we actually are.

But it's okay for things not to be okay. When life makes us start over, we must do it in a safe place. Never be so prideful that you miss a chance to be vulnerable with those who know you. There's something special about being able to show someone your scars.

Naomi's return home reminds us that we all must return to the source of our strength. And when you're seeking refuge, never forget the safest place there is—in the Master's arms.

JOURNAL

When was the last time you remember being happy, safe, or free?

What was it about that period that contributed to your joy?

Have you introduced people into your life who have drained you of your joy?

What are some things you like to do that make your heart smile?

How can you incorporate those into your everyday life?

PRAYER

Lord, somewhere along the way I got lost. I don't know how I got here or how I can make things better. I just know that I don't want to live like this anymore. God, help me to build my life with You as the foundation. I know that time and relationships will always add to my burden, but when it all gets to be too much, I hope You'll help me see where I went wrong. Even if that means starting all over. Amen.

DO WHAT YOU CAN

It's so easy to let rejection stop us from trying,
but you must be dedicated to survive.

Now there was a wealthy and influential man in Bethlehem named Boaz, who was a relative of Naomi's husband, Elimelech.

One day Ruth the Moabite said to Naomi, "Let me go out into the harvest fields to pick up the stalks of grain left behind by anyone who is kind enough to let me do it."

Naomi replied, "All right, my daughter, go ahead." So Ruth went out to gather grain behind the harvesters. And as it happened, she found herself working in a field that belonged to Boaz, the relative of her father-in-law, Elimelech.

RUTH 2:1-3 NLT

*J*oanne had her first child at twenty-eight. After an impressive collegiate career, including a year's study in Paris, she and her husband started a family. Nearly five months after the birth of her daughter, however, Joanne and her husband divorced. She had done everything "right," but her presumably perfect life hit rock bottom. She didn't have a job and was forced to live on government assistance.

Long before this detour on her journey, Joanne loved writing short stories. Maybe she couldn't fix her marriage, maybe her future was uncertain, but she knew one thing for sure: She could still write. Soon her stories grew into a full-length book. Rejected by twelve publishers before reaching millions of readers around the world, Joanne, better known as J. K. Rowling, is the mastermind behind Harry Potter.

We cannot allow rejection to convince us to stop trying. Whether it be in the pursuit of our heart's desires or the belief in our dreams, our dedication is what separates us from others. Ruth was not allowed to glean in the fields with the other women, but she didn't let the rejection stop her from doing what she could. It may have been the leftovers, but something was better than nothing. Sometimes what appears to be left over can become the seeds for future harvests. If you're committed to a new life, you have to be willing to keep going without seeing an immediate return.

Or think of it this way. Most mothers will tell you that the most exciting part of pregnancy is when they finally see their stomach swell with the new life inside. Before there are any outward signs of growth, their body has been making all these internal changes. Staying awake past seven feels like punishment. The smell of tacos makes them sick. And almost everyone seems to have a personal mission to get on their nerves in some way. . . . Well, okay, maybe that was just me. None of it matters, though, when your body starts welcoming the new life inside you. Suddenly, others can see that you aren't just being lazy, picky, or irritable. You are birthing something.

When circumstances restrict you from being able to do certain things, don't treat it as punishment. Just know that it's a part of your growing process. The common denominator between a pregnant woman whose body is no longer the same and a particular single mother whose "perfect life" fell apart is dedication to a new life.

Choose to believe that, in spite of your rejection or restrictions, there is hope for you yet. Ruth couldn't glean with the rest of the women. She already decided she couldn't go back to her homeland. So she made the best of her situation and did what she could. Don't be discouraged; what you see as restrictions could really just be preparation and protection.

JOURNAL

What was your first encounter with a major personal rejection?

What did you learn from it?

Did you give up after you were rejected? Why or why not?

What's keeping you from trying once again to pursue your destiny?

PRAYER

*God, help me to see that rejection is simply Your divine direction.
Thank You for closing the doors that weren't part of Your
plan. I'm grateful that You opened a window and made a
way of escape when I had chosen my will over Your own. I ask
that You cover me as I guard my heart from the infection of
disappointment. I trust that I'm not in this alone. Amen.*

You Never Know
Who's Watching

"Live your life in such a way that if someone lied about you,
no one would believe it."

—*based on 1 Peter 2:12*

Just then Boaz arrived from Bethlehem and greeted the harvesters, "The Lord be with you!"

"The Lord bless you!" they answered.

Boaz asked the overseer of his harvesters, "Who does that young woman belong to?"

RUTH 2:4–5

*H*ow many times have you watched the news as the camera pans to a person in an orange jumpsuit—their eyes bugged out, movements erratic, and voice shaky—and instantly you assume they're as guilty as they look? Or think about how some of our most sensational television shows revolve around criminal cases. Immediately, the audience determines whether the suspect is innocent or guilty based on how the alleged criminal looks. Sometimes right, sometimes wrong, the viewer plays a guessing game based largely on how a suspect reacts under pressure.

You may never be under that level of public scrutiny, but we've all found ourselves being judged by others. How you respond often reveals whether there is any validity in the accusations against you. You cannot control who judges you, but you can be responsible for portraying the most authentic version of yourself. It doesn't stop the judgment, but it allows others to see your truth whether they like it or not.

Ruth stood out not just by being a foreigner but also because of how confidently she conducted herself—despite how she may have felt inside. As Boaz stared from his favorite spot in the field, his eyes stopped on the stranger straggling behind the other gleaners. From where he stood, she just appeared to be a loner, a woman who didn't belong with the crowd.

Ruth didn't know she was being watched. As lonely and fearful as she may have been, her isolation became her platform. Ruth was more noticeable on her own than she ever would've been in the crowd. There's something to be said about not fitting in.

From the inside looking out, we wonder what's wrong with us. We feel self-conscious and wonder why others aren't willing to accept us for who we are. We think, *Is it my hair? Is it my weight? Am I not smart enough?* We view our separation as punishment, wondering what we did that landed us here and how we can fit in. From the inside we let our differences torment us until we no longer desire to belong. We accept that this may always be our fate and things will not get better. We allow struggle to rob us of our hope.

You never know what giving up on yourself teaches others about you. Be careful, especially in trials, to govern your actions with grace and hope. Your ability to maintain class in the midst of a storm is an indication of what you believe about yourself.

There's an old saying, "Never let them see you sweat." Notice it doesn't say, "Do not sweat at all." It just says you don't need to let the world see when the pressure is getting to you. Learn to vent in a safe place so that you can pull it together when it counts. In the safety of her home with Naomi, Ruth could acknowledge her fears. But when it was time to face the day, she greeted others with the strength poured into her at home.

Ruth's graceful tenacity made Boaz sit up and take notice.

Be careful how you handle this storm; you never know who's watching.

JOURNAL

Who is someone you currently admire? Why?
What is it about them that has earned your respect?

How has their journey affected your own?

What would someone learn about you if they saw you in
your weakest moment?

If you are the only reflection of Christ that people see,
would He be pleased with how you represent Him?

PRAYER

*As I strive to be more like You, I hope that You will help me
to remember my life is not my own. In anger, disappointment,
and frustration, I want to be able to represent Your sacrifice
on Calvary. Help me to look beyond myself and seek the grace
that will make You proud of how I handled my test. Amen.*

YOUR ENEMY BECOMES
YOUR FOOTSTOOL

Other people's gossip about you can often become the best
advertisement for your authenticity.

The foreman replied, "She is the young woman from Moab who came back with Naomi. She asked me this morning if she could gather grain behind the harvesters. She has been hard at work ever since, except for a few minutes' rest in the shelter."

Boaz went over and said to Ruth, "Listen, my daughter. Stay right here with us when you gather grain; don't go to any other fields. Stay right behind the young women working in my field. See which part of the field they are harvesting, and then follow them. I have warned the young men not to treat you roughly. And when you are thirsty, help yourself to the water they have drawn from the well."

RUTH 2:6–9 NLT

*Y*ears ago I heard a song in a movie trailer, and the lyrics, combined with the soulful rendering, made me want to be a better writer. Weird, I know. There was just something about this singer creating a sound that had never been heard before that made me want to create something special, too. My little secret, my creative muse, soon went from being music's best-kept secret to becoming the incomparable Adele.

Beloved for her talent and commitment to being her authentic self, she inspired me to remember that talent and authenticity can live in the same place. Adele was discovered after posting a few songs on MySpace. The news of her great talent spread until she could no longer go unnoticed. She could not be ignored. She didn't need all the hype of a marketing team and tabloid gossip to become a household name. People could feel who she really is just by listening to her music.

If we're true to ourselves, then we don't have to worry about what others may say about us. Our actions and authenticity will speak louder than anyone else's words. We have to realize that some people will always be tempted to misconstrue our actions and spread lies about us.

Ruth learned quickly that her arrival into a strange land acquired the attention of many. As a new convert, she may have faced some speculation on the validity of her faith. Perhaps they even questioned her motives. Why would a young woman stay with this aging, grief-stricken woman?

The rumors spread so rapidly that everyone knew her story before getting to know her. The conversations about her, whether idle chatter or malicious gossip, made her journey more difficult. It's one thing to struggle; it's another to struggle on stage.

Yet how could she have ever guessed that the town's gossiping about her would lead to her being blessed? Without even realizing it, they were giving information to the man who would change her life. Instead of judging her based on idle rumors, Boaz witnessed Ruth's determination firsthand. He saw for himself the kind of person she was.

Right before her eyes, Ruth's enemies became her footstool. Don't let the possibility of your name being tarnished keep you from doing right. If you're so busy defending yourself from idle rumors and salacious gossip, you won't have the energy to stay on your journey. If you dedicate all of your concentration to the whispers of others, how will you hear when He comes calling for you?

JOURNAL

How has your life been affected by gossip?

How has it deterred you from excelling in a particular area? How has it motivated you to pursue your goals?

Ruth found the strength to live in the face of gossip. How can you withstand your critics and find the strength to tell your own story?

If people are able to only see you and hear your story from others, what do you hope the combination says about you?

PRAYER

God, help me to remember that if I don't learn to live again, rumors will define me. I know You've placed too much inside of me for gossip to stop me. I trust You to take even my most shameful moment and use it to help me reach my destiny. I just pray You give me the grace to hold my head high when the whispers begin to weigh me down. Amen.

HE KNEW YOU BEFORE
HE BLESSED YOU

*Don't let rumors shame you
into believing God can't use you.*

At this, she bowed down with her face to the ground. She asked him, "Why have I found such favor in your eyes that you notice me—a foreigner?"

Boaz replied, "I've been told all about what you have done for your mother-in-law since the death of your husband—how you left your father and mother and your homeland and came to live with a people you did not know before. May the Lord repay you for what you have done. May you be richly rewarded by the Lord, the God of Israel, under whose wings you have come to take refuge."

RUTH 2:10-12

*N*ewly released convicts often forget what it's like to be free. Confined for so long, they don't remember how to function independently. They continue to think of themselves as nothing more than the verdict for their crimes. They assume others see them this way, and they themselves may not know how to define themselves apart from their past mistakes. And, unfortunately, many of them end up making the same mistakes again, only to return to confinement.

We may not be incarcerated, but we all experience this dilemma. And you know why our history repeats itself? Because instead of letting the past teach us, we allow it to define us. Either our obstacles in life hover over us forever or we find a way to climb on top of them and advance to the next level of our destiny. They either crush us from the burden of their weight or become the stepping stone, the launching pad, of our greatness.

When people recognize us but don't exactly remember how they know us, we use shared memories to jog their recollection. Oddly enough, though, when God does exceedingly, abundantly above all that we may ask or think, we begin to doubt whether He remembers who we really are. *I don't think you meant to give this to me,* we think. *I'm the one who wrote bad checks. I'm the one who got an abortion. I'm the one who got the DUI. I'm the one who told those lies. I'm the one who has that terrible secret.* We find all of these excuses for why we don't deserve to be blessed.

How long will you allow your past to shackle you?

When Ruth asked Boaz, "Why have I found such favor in your eyes that you notice me—a foreigner?" she gives us a peek into her mind-set. She had been keeping the faith, doing the right things, and becoming a stronger person, but a part of her still didn't believe she was worthy of being blessed. She assumed Boaz saw her as nothing more than a stranger, a woman from Moab who had wandered into Bethlehem. She received a tremendous opportunity, seemingly out of nowhere, and still didn't recognize it as her harvest.

In order to receive the blessings of God, we must quiet that voice inside of us that wonders, *Why me?* Ruth wanted to know why Boaz would bless a stranger; little did she know, he knew exactly who she was. When God uses someone to sow into your life, don't discredit it because you think they don't know you. God knows you and that's enough. He knows your struggle and still sees your worth. He knew you before He blessed you.

Don't miss out on your harvest by defining yourself by your past.

JOURNAL

What are you most ashamed of? Why?

What one decision in your past do you wish you could change?
What are the ongoing consequences of the mistake you made?

How has your shame changed you?

How can you use what broke you to help others?

PRAYER

*I know I am not the only one who has ever experienced this
shame, but still I can't move past this moment in my head.
I can't stop judging myself about what happened. God,
please take these thoughts and these memories and show me
how I can learn from the things that broke me. Amen.*

Surpass Them All

*The one who gets counted out, talked about,
and discredited can surpass them all.*

Then she said, "I have found favor in your sight, my lord, for you have comforted me and indeed have spoken kindly to your maidservant, though I am not like one of your maidservants."

At mealtime Boaz said to her, "Come here, that you may eat of the bread and dip your piece of bread in the vinegar." So she sat beside the reapers; and he served her roasted grain, and she ate and was satisfied and had some left.

RUTH 2:13-14 NASB

A part of me always wanted to be a serious athlete. I love the commitment and discipline athletes put into their training. My only problem is that this part of me is so small compared with the part that hates working out. Sure, I feel great afterward, I like the way I look, and my clothes fit better. But in the moment, I *hate* summoning the energy and making my body work so much harder than it wants. Maybe that's why I enjoy being a "couch coach" so much.

A couch coach is someone who sits at home on their couch and yells through the TV to coach their favorite athletes and teams. Honestly, I don't really know that much about sports, but every now and then I do get lucky. One year we were all watching the Olympics as a family, and we decided to try to guess the winners. I was on a pretty impressive streak until it was time for the track and field events. After briefly leaving the room, I returned just as a new race started, so I picked the obvious choice—the runner currently in the lead.

The timer was ticking and fans were erupting with cheers for the love of country and sports. Then I noticed a speck on the television screen. Way in the distant background of the track, something was moving crazy fast. It came closer and closer into the camera range until I realized it was another runner. Gaining momentum and speed, within minutes he was battling for the number-one spot. He came out of nowhere yet surpassed them all.

Ruth knew what it was like to come from behind before moving ahead. Gleaning the fields behind the paid reapers, she likely had been judged and dismissed with an eye roll and was merely being tolerated by them. It wasn't long, however, before Ruth found herself enjoying dinner with Boaz, the owner of the land.

The one they had counted out had now surpassed them all.

It's not too late. It may look like you're behind now. It may appear to others that you won't be able to become much or accomplish anything. But God has seen your work. He has seen your dedication to fighting back against life's blows. Don't be tricked into believing that, if others don't endorse you, God can't use you. In His infinite wisdom and grace, He has no need to get approval from others to bless you.

You may be toward the back of the pack, but the race isn't over yet.

JOURNAL

Do you feel like you're behind in your progress compared with others?

Are you giving your best effort to win the race, or has life taken away your endurance?

Ruth humbly gathered what was left over from the ladies who gleaned ahead of her. It wasn't ideal, but it was what she had to do to survive. She didn't allow pride to stand in her way. Can God trust you with your current position?

What do you need to do today to stay in the race?

PRAYER

Please allow me to see that even when I'm not where I want to be, I am exactly where You need me to be. I pray that I can accept when it's time for me to stay behind, and trust You when You take me higher. Most importantly, God, no matter what my current position may be, give me the strength to endure this race. Amen.

There Will Be an Overflow

Before, Ruth was gleaning whatever was left behind;
now she had more than enough.

And when she rose up to glean, Boaz commanded his young men, saying, "Let her glean even among the sheaves, and do not reproach her. Also let grain from the bundles fall purposely for her; leave it that she may glean, and do not rebuke her."

RUTH 2:15–16 NKJV

*L*ike most women, I enjoy shopping for new clothes. A little retail therapy can make your day brighter—as long as there's room for it in your budget. It would be great to buy some shoes, a couple nice bags, and a few outfits to match instead of paying bills. But the clothes do us no good if we don't have a home to store them, lights to see them, or water to wash them. So we learn to cut back on our wants and focus on our needs.

When I start complaining about the areas of lack in my life, however, I always remember one of my favorite Scriptures: "You have been faithful over a few things, I will make you ruler over many things" (Matthew 25:23 NKJV). You can't be faithful with what you have if you're always thinking about what you wish you had. We must strive to show God that we can be trusted with both blessings and struggles. Without trials, we could not fully appreciate our blessings. Ultimately, we value what we must work for.

When Ruth first came to the fields, she started gleaning behind the other ladies. What they had overlooked or been too full to carry became hers. Sure, it may not have been as much as they had, but it was hers. Once again, Ruth proves to us there's blessing in persevering. She refused to let the odds dictate her future. Boaz then ordered not only that she be allowed to glean with the other women but that they leave handfuls of grain for her.

Our God is a God of more than enough. He won't just bless you; He'll blow your mind. Will you let Him?

Boaz directed his servants to give Ruth special treatment. Before he noticed her, she was gleaning whatever was left behind; now she had more than enough. Ruth went from wondering what she and Naomi would eat that day to experiencing abundance.

As God did for Ruth, we can trust that He will see we've been faithful and can be trusted with overflow. When God promotes you, He's going to give you special treatment. Where you once struggled, now you will have abundance.

God is waiting to create an overflow in your areas of lack. Before He can bless you, though, He must know that He can trust you. Be grateful for what you have. Sure, we all have areas in our lives that we wish we could improve, but we can't afford to invest in worry. Make the best out of what you do have; then let God do the rest.

JOURNAL

Identify the areas of lack in your life.

Have you shown yourself to be faithful over those areas in your life?

Have you ever been trusted with overflow (extra money, time, freedom)? How did you handle it?

Ruth did *everything* she could to survive. Are you using all of whatever you have left from your despair to make tomorrow a better day? What could you be doing differently?

PRAYER

God, help me not to dwell on the pain that I felt, the tears I cried, or the memories that won't fade. Lord, only You can take my not enough and turn it into more than I ever imagined. So here I am, God, turning it over to You. I don't know what You can do with these pieces, but I know it's better than anything I could do. Amen.

MAKE OTHERS BELIEVE

Your ability to keep the faith, despite all
that has happened, will help others believe.

So she gleaned in the field until evening. Then she beat out what she had gleaned, and it was about an ephah of barley. She took it up and went into the city, and her mother-in-law saw what she had gleaned. She also took it out and gave Naomi what she had left after she was satisfied.

Her mother-in-law then said to her, "Where did you glean today and where did you work? May he who took notice of you be blessed." So she told her mother-in-law with whom she had worked and said, "The name of the man with whom I worked today is Boaz." Naomi said to her daughter-in-law, "May he be blessed of the Lord who has not withdrawn his kindness to the living and to the dead." Again Naomi said to her, "The man is our relative, he is one of our closest relatives."

RUTH 2:17–20 NASB

*I*t wasn't until I reached adulthood that I understood the impact of parenting. More than the family vacations or the stories before bed, my most treasured memories of my parents were the things they didn't say. The generational core values of who I am weren't instilled through verbal communication. I watched them, and watching them taught me.

As their own parents aged, I watched my father and mother care, guide, and protect my grandparents all the way to their final stages of life. It is the most profound memory for me because it taught me that the true sign of gratitude is service. My parents showed their appreciation for the sacrifices their parents had made by serving them when they could no longer help themselves.

I now try to show my parents my own gratitude in whatever small ways I can. Whether it's cooking dinner, running errands, or pulling back their covers for bed, I try to show them what I have witnessed: Anytime God blesses them, they serve in return.

Naomi was convinced God had cursed her. When God blessed Ruth, it helped Naomi to believe again. When Ruth was finished gleaning, she took what she had accrued and shared it with Naomi. When Naomi saw that Ruth's faithfulness had been rewarded, she dared to believe again. Maybe God had not forgotten her after all. Ruth's blessing helped Naomi's joy return.

Inspiring someone is such a different feeling than making a friend, connecting with them intellectually, or being able to make them laugh. When you inspire someone, it means something you said or did made him or her want to be better. Ruth was just trying to survive. She had once pledged her life and love to her husband, Mahlon. Even after his death, she was committed to making sure what was left of him, through her relationship with Naomi, was nurtured. Ruth decided she would do whatever it took to survive the challenges that come with making a commitment.

Who knows why God chose you to bear the weight that you do. But perhaps you aren't struggling just for you. Your ability to remain faithful in spite of pain can help someone—but only if you show them. Don't be so obsessed with an image of perfection that you miss an opportunity to show where grace abides in your life. You never know whom you might inspire—or when they might in turn inspire you.

JOURNAL

How has your life been affected by the sacrifices of those around you?

Do you let the success or failures of your family and friends inspire you or intimidate you?

How have you shown others what God has done in your life?

How could sharing your testimony protect someone who hears you?

PRAYER

Lord, if I knew my story could spare someone from what I experienced, I would share it with Your people. I'm just so afraid of being judged and criticized. God, give me the wisdom not to throw my pearls among swine. Instead, allow me to save them and share them with those who can see the worth in my struggle. Amen.

Extra Protection

Not only will God bless you, but He will protect you
along with the blessing He's entrusted to you.

Then Ruth the Moabite said, "He even said to me, 'Stay with my workers until they finish harvesting all my grain.'"

Naomi said to Ruth her daughter-in-law, "It will be good for you, my daughter, to go with the women who work for him, because in someone else's field you might be harmed."

So Ruth stayed close to the women of Boaz to glean until the barley and wheat harvests were finished. And she lived with her mother-in-law.

RUTH 2:21-23

*T*he Secret Service has many responsibilities. Among them are protecting the president, vice president, their families, cabinet members, and other designated individuals. Recently, Congress passed a law that allows former presidents to have Secret Service protection for life. As the world seems to become increasingly more dangerous, I see why it is necessary to provide lifetime security to those who were elected to the highest office in government, even after they leave the White House.

Just like we see with such political figures, when God elevates us, He also protects us. Boaz had given Ruth unprecedented access to his fields. Within one day she went from gleaning what was left over to having more than enough. In addition, Boaz made sure not only that she received plenty of grain but that she would not be harmed or threatened. Ruth did not have to worry about losing her gifts by being attacked, robbed, raped, or disrespected. Boaz was her protector as well as her provider.

This passage of Ruth reminds us that God doesn't bless us without protecting us. Too often we believe we're ready for our blessing, but when we receive it, we instantly become afraid of losing it. As if God may not bless us more than once, we allow fear to make us stingy. We must remember that He doesn't provide for us and bless us today only to pull it all away from us tomorrow. He gives us the protection we need to maintain our blessings.

The same God who protected Ruth and Naomi as they journeyed from Moab to Bethlehem was with them when He elevated them from just enough to overflow. His protection and blessings run parallel. Do not let the insecurity of something being taken away cause you to hold too tightly to an object and, ultimately, let go of God. Similarly, sometimes we may need to let go of what He has given us so that He can enlarge our blessing and give us even more. Remember, He has promised that if we serve Him—not things or people—no weapon formed against us shall prosper.

God doesn't give us favor without protection. If He trusted you enough to give it to you, He'll provide the security it requires to guard His investment. Don't become stingy or greedy. Instead, remember, "He who began a good work in you will carry it on to completion until the day of Christ Jesus" (Philippians 1:6).

JOURNAL

What is the most valuable thing you have ever lost?

How has your perspective on the loss changed over time?

How would your life be different if you had never experienced this loss?

Have you allowed what you lost to make you better or bitter?

PRAYER

God, help me to see that everything I've lost helped make me better. It may have hurt, and I may have been broken. But I know that if You saw fit for me to lose now, it's so that I can win later. Help me to believe You still see me. I truly want to live again, but I'm scared. I'm afraid of losing again. I need to believe You'll protect all that You have invested in me. Amen.

THE BEGINNING
OF THE END

*We must dedicate ourselves to gathering the leftovers
and keeping the faith, knowing that if God did it for her,
He'll do it for us.*

"Blessed be he of the Lord, who has not forsaken His kindness
to the living and the dead!"

RUTH 2:20 NKJV

*I*n the beginning of chapter 2, we meet a dedicated Ruth, determined to keep her faith as well as her commitment to her mother-in-law. When the chapter ends, Ruth is on the verge of a breakthrough. After the devastation of losing the men in her life, traveling to a new city, facing gossip, trying to take care of Naomi, and struggling with discouragement, she finds her fate changing quickly. As her trials come to an end, she learns there are blessings waiting for her and protection covering her.

This second chapter is my favorite in the book of Ruth. Within twenty-three verses, Ruth's life begins to turn completely around. This chapter relates the events that seem like the turning point in her story. She went from a mind-set of simply surviving to an unexpected collision with destiny. How could she have known that the tears she cried, the weight she carried, and the rumors spread about her were all just preparation? How could she have known that what was taken away was simply making room for what was to come?

When life becomes too much to bear, it's easy to become stagnant. We're tempted to obsess about what we've lost and allow our bitterness to fester. But this is the very time we must dedicate ourselves to gathering the leftovers and keeping the faith. You must choose to believe that if God did it for Ruth, He'll do it for you. You're coming out of the storm. The torrential rain has turned to a slow drizzle. Thunder rumbles, but only as a distant echo of the danger it once threatened.

Keep holding on to His promise and see what's next.

That thing that hurts you, the people you lost along the way, and the moments when you decided to push instead of giving up are all preparation. Look over your life—the choices you made and the shame you feel may never go away. Aren't you ready to see what God can do? Then just keep walking, step-by-step, day-by-day.

Ruth's commitment to walk with God is the only reason she was on course to collide with destiny. Collisions hurt. They cause injuries and create pain, but the insurance that comes with God reminds us that everything that was damaged can be restored and replaced. Whether God is just making a few minor repairs in your life or totaling out your dreams so you can experience His will, don't shy away from the pain of collision.

As Ruth learned, it may be the only way you discover your destiny.

JOURNAL

The book of Ruth begins with death, but at the end of chapter 2 we see obvious signs of new life. What has to die in your life so that you can live?

Death brings grief and grief brings pain. Birth brings new life, but it also brings pain. How are you using your pain? Are you creating something new or still grieving what could have been?

If things turned around for you overnight, what would your pain have taught you that you will never forget?

Write a letter about your darkest pain. Write about how it affected your life. Describe any regret or shame you carried.

Imagine yourself free from the feelings you wrote about. Healed from the pain that haunts you. What does that girl look like? How has she become better? What makes her smile?

You can be that girl. You are on the road to a better you. Just like Ruth, your willingness to open your heart means you're on the verge of a breakthrough.

PRAYER

God, thank You for this breaking. Thank You for the pain and the tears. I'm thankful because You trusted me with this pain, grateful because here I am now, looking back and thanking You. Lord, I'm asking You to use these broken pieces to make me better. Help me to become wiser and stronger. I don't know what's in store for me, but I know I don't want to do it without You. Amen.

IT'S TIME TO TRY AGAIN

There will be moments after hurt and heartache
when we must make the decision to try again.

One day Naomi said to Ruth, "My daughter, it's time that I found a permanent home for you, so that you will be provided for. Boaz is a close relative of ours, and he's been very kind by letting you gather grain with his young women. Tonight he will be winnowing barley at the threshing floor. Now do as I tell you—take a bath and put on perfume and dress in your nicest clothes. Then go to the threshing floor, but don't let Boaz see you until he has finished eating and drinking. Be sure to notice where he lies down; then go and uncover his feet and lie down there. He will tell you what to do."

RUTH 3:1–4 NLT

*M*y mother underwent knee surgery, and as part of her recovery, she spent a few days in the hospital's rehabilitation facility. While visiting her there, I overheard a physical trainer telling another patient, a recent amputee, that the only way he would learn to use his prosthesis was if he tried. Evidently, the patient had been refusing to attempt to walk for some time. The trainer's frustration was beginning to show as he realized the hospital would eventually send the patient home if he continued to refuse his rehabilitation.

Instantly, I thought of my first real heartbreak and how hard it was for me to dare loving again. There are some pains so deep that we never want to try again. When you lose a part of yourself, it's hard to imagine you can continue to live as if something isn't missing. Sure, the patient's leg had been replaced with a prosthetic that would allow him to function, but he had to make the decision to try again.

It's one thing to be afraid of the unknown; it's another for our known experiences to inhibit us. You see, the patient didn't hate his prosthetic. He wasn't afraid of his trainer. The recovery work wasn't what made him despondent. The patient couldn't even fully evaluate those things because he couldn't escape the memory of what had hurt him and what he had lost.

Having worked on many cases, the trainer knew something the patient did not. If the patient dares to try, he learns that a prosthetic can become just as functional as his lost limb. It doesn't diminish the loss, but it does allow him to move forward. It's a choice of the will to illuminate the darkness of grief with a spark of hope.

Naomi's faith was restored because of Ruth's commitment to survival. In exchange, Naomi wanted to remind Ruth that the time had come for her to be restored, too. They had both been devastated, but notice that hidden within the word *devastate* is the word *state*. If you've ever driven coast to coast across our country, you know you have to go through a lot of states. When we go through a state of heartbreak, it's important for us to remember that our condition was not meant to keep us from reaching our divine destination.

Do not make devastation your permanent dwelling place. Instead, allow it to be a temporary place on your journey to recovery. The only way to escape your state of pain is to move. It's time to try again. Just as the patient must choose whether or not to allow the pain of what happened to keep him from trying, you, too, must decide whether to be constrained by agony or propelled by hope.

JOURNAL

When Ruth had to start over with Naomi, she had to make several adjustments along the way. Through it all, she also learned many things about herself. She learned to do with less. Through keeping her commitment to Naomi, she learned she had character. Her dedication to gleaning the leftovers showed her humility. If you look back and focus on something other than the pain, you'll see you're wiser and stronger now than you were before.

List three positive things you learned about yourself through your pain.

How have those lessons changed your outlook on life?

What are some small changes you can make now to help continue the starting-over process?

PRAYER

Lord, help me to see that I have the strength to try again. I may have been hurt, but I am stronger than I was before. I don't want my pain to be in vain. I want to use these lessons to reach my destiny. Clear my mind so that I can quiet the doubts and fears of my past. I want to be free when You say it's time to try again. Amen.

DAY 16

RESPECT THOSE WHO CAME BEFORE YOU

*There is wisdom for your journey
in listening to the wise counsel of others.*

And she said to her, "All that you say to me I will do." So she went down to the threshing floor and did according to all that her mother-in-law instructed her.

RUTH 3:5–6 NKJV

I'm at the age where I now realize that most of my parents' advice, comments, and guidance have been right all along. It's been a slow journey that began when I was a child, veered off track when I was a teenager, and has returned to the illumination of their wisdom as I've entered adulthood. More times than not, when my parents tried to warn me I was playing with fire, it wasn't until my skin was scorched that I conceded they were right.

Finally tired of receiving burns, I started listening. It didn't just stop there, though; the people whose opinions I once ignored have become the ones I now often seek out. When I first decided to purchase a home, I presented my plans to both my mom and dad. I wanted their advice on whether I was thinking things through clearly or needed to make some changes. I didn't want them to tell me what to do, but I needed them to share their wisdom gleaned from experience.

God places people in our lives who know us and love us enough to tell us the truth. Even if the truth makes us uncomfortable or upset, we mustn't ignore the words of the wise. Wisdom comes through experience, and experience through living. Why deny the ability to take a small peek into the future by ignoring the advice of those who went before you? Certainly, we all have our own struggles and mistakes to make, but ultimately we can spare ourselves a lot of trouble by simply listening.

On the way from Moab back to Bethlehem, Naomi told Ruth not to stay with her. The older woman tried to convince her daughter-in-law that life would be much easier if she returned to her homeland. Ruth listened, then made a decision for herself. Their circumstances changed, and once again Naomi gave Ruth advice—but this time Ruth listened and heeded what she heard. Naomi didn't decide to stop giving advice just because Ruth didn't take it previously. Naomi respected Ruth's right to make a decision about her life, even if she didn't agree with it.

It's important that we take a moment to at least listen to those who are trying to help us. You don't have to follow their advice or agree with everything they say, but make the decision to let other trusted individuals challenge your thought process. If we are not challenged, we cannot learn.

JOURNAL

Name three people you truly respect.

How have you been influenced by their lives?

How will you use their influences on your own journey of self-discovery?

How can you use your story to help soothe or counsel someone who's hurt in the same way you are?

PRAYER

God, ignite a light inside of me that will lead others to You. May my life be a representation of Your power to mend the broken. I pray that others look at my heart and see that Your light is capable of shining through the darkest of hurts. Thank You for allowing such strong people to go ahead of me so that I may use their shoulders to reach higher heights. Amen.

BE VULNERABLE

*There will be moments when others reveal their vulnerability
and you're invited to let down your guard with them.
We all need a place of shelter so that we can provide
the same for others.*

When Boaz had finished eating and drinking and was in good spirits, he went over to lie down at the far end of the grain pile. Ruth approached quietly, uncovered his feet and lay down. In the middle of the night something startled the man; he turned—and there was a woman lying at his feet!

"Who are you?" he asked.

"I am your servant Ruth," she said. "Spread the corner of your garment over me, since you are a guardian-redeemer of our family."

RUTH 3:7-9

*T*he older my siblings and I have become, the more trust we've gained from our parents. There's something so strange and wonderful about having the people who once told you what to do occasionally ask you what *they* should do. The dynamic has changed from my parents always giving directions to their seeking and respecting my opinions.

It's an incredible gift to be trusted with the unguarded pieces of who a person really is. Especially when that person is someone you admire and emulate as your teacher or mentor. In these moments we have the opportunity to take the relationship to a new level of maturity by matching their vulnerability with our own.

When Ruth goes to lie at Boaz's feet, he is unguarded and vulnerable. After having a festive evening with plenty of drinks and merriment, he has finally allowed himself to sleep. So imagine how startled he must be to find Ruth lying at his feet.

And consider the risk Ruth is taking. After life robbed her of her plans, she was forced to bury her husband, leave her hometown, and create a new life. Ruth had allowed survival to toughen her. Yet in this moment she matches Boaz's physical vulnerability with her emotional one. She needs a refuge. She requests Boaz to take her under his wing. Like a baby bird unprepared to face the world alone, Ruth wants Boaz to protect her.

This is an intimate moment of transparency for both of them. Boaz, a powerful businessman who appears to have it all together, is caught physically defenseless. Ruth, a strong woman determined to survive and not be beaten down by life, admits she's weary.

As my siblings and I grew older, we began to spread our own wings. No longer in need of constant covering, we've matured enough to occasionally provide refuge for our parents. As my parents began to entrust us with the whispers of their heart, we advanced from being just their children. We now get to provide a place of shelter and rest for them.

As this passage of Ruth demonstrates, everyone—no matter how strong or how weak—needs relationships in which they can rest and be vulnerable. Sure, you can cook dinner, do the laundry, punch the clock, take the classes, care for your parents, balance the checkbook, counsel your friends, and still have time to prepare for tomorrow. But every now and then, you must trust someone with the vulnerable side of you.

Remove the cape, take off the mask, and allow yourself to be human again. Yes, you can keep it moving. But you know a part of you is no longer strong enough to hold everything together. It's time to admit you need covering.

JOURNAL

When you're upset, who's the one person
who can calm you down?

What is it they do that relaxes you?

How has this relationship shaped how you handle
other people when they're angry?

How are your actions when handling another's
vulnerability a reflection of Christ's love?

PRAYER

*Please teach me the balanced dance of grace and mercy. May I
provide a flicker of hope in a person's darkest hour. I pray You give
me the perfect wisdom to speak to the heart of the matter. And
may I be as gentle with others as You have been with me. Amen.*

Your Blessing
Is in Your Obedience

*Sometimes what you can do and
what you should do are completely different.*

Then he said, "May you be blessed of the Lord, my daughter.
You have shown your last kindness to be better than the first
by not going after young men, whether poor or rich. Now, my
daughter, do not fear. I will do for you whatever you ask, for
all my people in the city know that you are a woman of excel-
lence. Now it is true I am a close relative; however, there is a
relative closer than I. Remain this night, and when morning
comes, if he will redeem you, good; let him redeem you. But
if he does not wish to redeem you, then I will redeem you, as
the Lord lives. Lie down until morning."

RUTH 3:10–13 NASB

*R*ecently I was on this diet. Not sure which one, but I know I stayed hungry. I mean, technically I was eating enough, but I couldn't shake the notion that if something wasn't fried, it wasn't good. So I had thrown away anything in my house that could possibly tempt me to break my diet. Then one day, after spending the afternoon with their favorite aunt, my children returned home with McDonald's Happy Meals. Any other day I wouldn't have cared, but that day I had just seen a commercial for the fast-food chain and suddenly the nuggets looked delicious.

I wanted the taste but not the calories, so (don't judge me, okay?) I chewed the chicken nugget, just for the taste, and then spit it out. (You're judging. . . . Stop!) Sad, I know. Afterward, I especially appreciated why my trainer had told me to throw away all the junk food in my house. It's so much easier to be obedient when you don't have any other options.

With a deceased husband and bitter mother-in-law, Ruth suddenly had plenty of options. She had at least a couple good reasons to go her own way and do whatever she pleased. And Boaz recognized that she had other options. Still, Ruth chose to obey the customs of her new land. Boaz commended her for keeping her commitment to her deceased husband even though he was no longer there to witness it.

The true measure of a person is revealed when they have options. Do you tithe on your paycheck or buy an extra pair of shoes? Do you use your sphere of influence to help build up others or just to build up yourself? Do you act the same way when you travel for your job as you do at home?

Who are you when no one is watching?

We make life so much more difficult than it has to be, all because we make God an option instead of a priority. If you're going to continue to grow in Christ, you must remove from your life anything that will distract you from Him.

The world allows us numerous opportunities to choose between our flesh and our God. We don't always choose correctly, but God is gracious enough to take all of our missteps and incorporate them into His master vision. Don't let a disobedient past prohibit you from having an ordained future. It's only on the road of obedience that we collide with our destiny—not when we're trailblazing off on our own.

JOURNAL

When is the last time you sacrificed something
you wanted for something you needed?

What motivated you to make the sacrifice?

What are some areas where you wish you had
the discipline to make a change in your life?

What's keeping you from making this change?

PRAYER

*God, help me to surrender fully to Your will. I want to give
myself away to be used for Your purpose. I need Your hand
on my life. Help me to see that You have greater things
in store for me than even I can imagine. Amen.*

THOSE WHO LOVE YOU WILL PROTECT YOU

When you value someone, you're careful how you handle,
protect, and cover them.

So Ruth lay at Boaz's feet until the morning, but she got up before it was light enough for people to recognize each other. For Boaz had said, "No one must know that a woman was here at the threshing floor."

RUTH 3:14 NLT

*B*efore little girls turn into adult women, we are taught to approach one particular type of man with great caution. My father warned me. My mother warned me. My brothers and older girlfriends warned me. Beware of the man who considers you a conquest and brags to all of his friends about adding you to his list. Even men who don't seem to be players can sometimes betray your reputation by disregarding how things appear to other people. This kind of man cares more about his ego than about your integrity and ignores his responsibility to shelter your heart.

On the other hand, someone who truly cares for you is always thinking about your best interests. After their divinely appointed rendezvous, Boaz told Ruth that no one must know she was there with him that night. He is fully aware of the implications that could arise from their late-night meeting. Even though he knew nothing immoral or inappropriate happened, he was savvy enough to know what it might look like to others.

Boaz protected Ruth's image. Even in his excitement about their possible future, Boaz had enough foresight to look ahead and protect her from any potential disgrace. After all, Ruth had worked very hard to build a reputable name in her new home. Despite the initial rumors, she was well respected in the town because of her faithfulness to Naomi and her dedicated work ethic.

There's something to be said about someone who doesn't just understand you but also protects your worth. Those who love you don't just see you as an opportunity; they see you as a gift. When you value someone, you're careful how you handle, protect, and cover them.

Boaz had spent the evening with one of Bethlehem's most intriguing women, yet he still desired to protect what they shared. As a man of character, he cared more about the long-term view—their future together—than just the present moment. As the sun began to shed light on the mysteries of the evening, Boaz made sure their secret would remain safe. Perhaps he knew that premature exposure could ruin their budding relationship.

Wait for the Boaz in your life before you reveal the tenderness of your heart. If you aren't careful, you'll give yourself to someone who shares your most vulnerable moments with the world. You are far too valuable to give yourself away for bragging rights. Those who really love you will protect you from the prying eyes of the world.

JOURNAL

Do you have someone in your life who can help make you think outside of the box?

How well do you receive input from your loved ones? Do you question their motives or know they have your best interests at heart?

Before Ruth could even open her mouth to consider what others would think of her late departure, Boaz was covering her. He was a few steps ahead of her. Do you have people in your life who are a few steps ahead of you?

How can you begin to invest wisdom and love into your relationships so that you are covering them?

PRAYER

I need to have more wisdom in my life, God. I have no time for the distractions of trivial things; I'm preparing for my destiny. Lord, give me the spirit of discernment so I can remove anything or anyone distracting me from my destiny. Cover me with the gift of Your wisdom. Amen.

RELATIONSHIPS
ARE INVESTMENTS

"The worst regret we have in life,
is not for the wrong things we did, but for the thousands
of right things we did, for the wrong people."

—*Unknown*

Also he said, "Bring the shawl that is on you and hold it." And when she held it, he measured six ephahs of barley, and laid it on her. Then she went into the city.

When she came to her mother-in-law, she said, "Is that you, my daughter?" Then she told her all that the man had done for her.

RUTH 3:15–16 NKJV

*D*uring my sophomore year of college, I had a schedule that gave me a lot of extra time off. Enough time, in fact, that I decided to get a part-time job. After searching the online student community for leads, I finally found a job that would allow me to tutor middle-school-aged children in the afternoons.

To say the least, I was excited. It wasn't that it was my first job. Growing up in church, I was used to working with kids all the time. Actually, it's more accurate to say that in church I was always volunteering, because the pay was love and hugs. So now I would actually have a paying job!

Because of my start date, I was told I would have to wait three weeks for my first paycheck. That was fine with me, though; a three-week wait was better than no paycheck at all. Around midnight the day of my scheduled direct deposit, I refreshed my computer screen dozens of times. There it was—all $304.87 of my first paycheck!

I was brimming with excitement! I was so proud of my first check and so excited about my first real paying job that I wanted to go celebrate. So I planned dinner with some of my friends at one of our favorite restaurants. Scheduled a nail appointment. Ran to the mall. And still had time to stop by Target to grab a couple of movies just in case the girls stayed the night.

You guessed it: I got paid Friday and my money was gone by

Sunday. I learned very quickly that if I didn't start spending my money wisely, I would have nothing to show for it. As I came into adulthood, I learned the power of investing.

In its simplest form, when you invest something, whether it's your time or finances, you do so expecting a return. That's why we *spend* time and *spend* money. We give something away in hopes that what we receive back is greater than what we put in.

For a businessman like Boaz, giving away six measures of barley to Ruth was an investment. Though she had made herself available to him, he insisted on following the protocol of the land and seeking the relative that had the first right to marry her. While there were no strings attached to his gift of grain, Boaz hoped that he was creating an investment in his future with Ruth. He wanted her to know he was serious about wanting to marry her.

God invests in us the same way. Each day we're here on earth is God-given time, a divine investment. We have an opportunity to honor His investment with our mind, gifts, service, and spirit. My prayer is that we find the courage to fight whatever blocks our efforts to give God the maximum return on His investment. No matter what your challenges might be, remember that if God is still investing air into your lungs, then He still has a destiny for you.

JOURNAL

Where do you invest the majority of your time and finances?

What do your investments say about you?

What have others invested in you?

How do you remain patient to wait on the return of your investment?

PRAYER

God, I know You have placed so much inside of me. Please help me see that there is life after my pain. I want to believe that I can still give You a return on Your investment. I just need the strength to move past this moment so I can live again. Amen.

WAIT PATIENTLY

When you're right on the edge of a breakthrough,
expect your patience to be tested.

Then she told her everything Boaz had done for her and added, "He gave me these six measures of barley, saying, 'Don't go back to your mother-in-law empty-handed.'"

Then Naomi said, "Wait, my daughter, until you find out what happens. For the man will not rest until the matter is settled today."

RUTH 3:16–18

No one informed me that buying a house is like playing "Hurry Up and Wait." Yes, it's a real game. It's the same game some hair stylists play, as well as doctors and dentists. They tell you to be on time or they'll cancel your appointment. So you arrive on time and then have to sit and wait thirty minutes at least.

Had I known this game is at the essence of becoming a home-owner, I would have been better prepared. But I didn't, so I've emailed my lender every other day to check the status of my loan. And every other day I've received the same answer: "It could be any day now, so just be patient." Hurry up and wait.

The mortgage company doesn't understand. I have Pinterest boards full of my favorite designs. I've found the perfect bed for the master bedroom, and the bed I want for my son, Malachi, has just gone on sale. I'm excited to start nesting, but the process of waiting has become so nerve-racking.

After almost a month, I received the preapproval for my loan and put a home under contract. As I write this, another two months have gone by, and I still have no status update on my final loan and when we'll close. I'm within reach of my goals, so close I can brush it with my fingertips, but not there yet.

This in-between time when you're almost-but-not-yet can be the most frustrating time of any process. It's the moment when you can see your goal in front of you but just aren't where you want to be yet.

This is when we must remember that Ruth 3:18 sounds a lot like Philippians 1:6: "Being confident of this, that he who began a good work in you will carry it on to completion until the day of Christ Jesus." God will not give up on you. In church we say, "I don't believe He's brought me this far to leave me."

These are the moments when our faith becomes the only thing we have to hold on to. You did the best you could with what you were given. God blessed your work to go to the next level, and now you must see if there is even more than you dreamed of waiting for you. Ruth set out on a journey of survival and collided with her destiny. She didn't begin the process hoping to be married to the man who owned the field. She worked to better herself, and through this effort she was blessed and able to bless others.

Can you be patient while He does His good work in you?

With my home loan, I have turned in all the paper work, answered every question, and faxed every document. There's nothing else I can do but leave it in God's hands.

When you've done all you can do, rest your mind and be at peace. You've sown all the right seeds. You've tried to right as many wrongs as you can. You continue being the best wife you can be, the best mother you can be, the best friend. Now it's time for God to do the rest. Don't give up because your harvest hasn't come quickly. The most rewarding investments take time to grow.

JOURNAL

How have you made peace with what hurt you?

What was your role in the hurt? How has your role now changed?

Did you seek forgiveness from yourself or others for your part?

Have you done all that you can do?

PRAYER

God, help me to humble myself to take a look on the inside. A large part of me was taken, broken from me by life. I don't want to lose anything else unless it goes to You. Your will be done, not mine. Give me the patience to wait on Your blessing. I'm ready to be restored and find the peace in my collision. Amen.

GOD WILL PUT LIKE-MINDED PEOPLE IN YOUR LIFE

*You don't have to chase people down or convince them to be in
your life. God will bring the right people at the perfect time.*

Meanwhile Boaz went up to the town gate and sat down there just as the guard-ian-redeemer he had mentioned came along. Boaz said, "Come over here, my friend, and sit down." So he went over and sat down.

Boaz took ten of the elders of the town and said, "Sit here," and they did so. Then he said to the guardian-redeemer, "Naomi, who has come back from Moab, is selling the piece of land that belonged to our relative Elimelek. I thought I should bring the matter to your attention and suggest that you buy it in the presence of these seated here and in the presence of the elders of my people. If you will redeem it, do so. But if you will not, tell me, so I will know. For no one has the right to do it except you, and I am next in line."

"I will redeem it," he said.

RUTH 4:1-4

*I*t's been bittersweet to see how some of my friendships have changed over time. And it's been especially surprising to see the way friends' lives and lifestyles change as well. Everyone grows at a different rate. Often when we change for the better, we want people in our lives who are like-minded so that we can be motivated to stay the course.

Had you asked Ruth about her BFF back in Moab, she might have said it was her sister-in-law Orpah. We can't know this for sure, but it seems plausible. After all, they married into the same family, they came from the same land, and they spent plenty of time with each other.

When Orpah decided to stay in Moab, Ruth chose not to stay with her. Had Ruth stayed there, she never would have learned what she was really made of. Staying was fine for Orpah, but Ruth wanted more. There comes a time in life when we are ready to go to the next level. We must embrace the reality that everyone cannot go with us.

Orpah and Ruth did not have to quarrel to separate. They simply understood that their destinies were no longer tied to each other. So often we decide we will pursue our dream if someone else lands their dream job. Or we'll wait to go back to school until our friends also have the money to enroll. We don't want to better ourselves until others can handle the better us.

You cannot let your life be dictated by the reaction of others, though. Ultimately God has preordained your future, and He doesn't need the lives of your friends to parallel everything He has planned for you. Don't handcuff someone to your dream. They don't have to believe with you or cheer for you if God is with you.

You may have to spend some time alone while you find your way, but there are lessons in that, too. Ruth strived to live a life of integrity and commitment. She did what was right even if it meant it would hurt. Whether gleaning the leftovers in the field or consoling a bitter Naomi during her most difficult days, Ruth proved she was dedicated to the process.

Boaz knew he didn't have the first claim to marry Ruth, so he followed the protocol. How fitting that without her even realizing it, God had brought someone into her life who had the same level of commitment to integrity. By the time Boaz approached the other kinsman, Boaz had already shown interest in Ruth. He had invested in her and had firsthand knowledge of her virtue. But he knew he had to do the right thing even at the risk of losing her.

You don't have to chase people down or convince them to be in your life. God will bring the right people at the perfect time. Don't spend a lifetime holding yourself back because others do not want to go with you. If it comes down to following them or pursuing your destiny, make the right decision.

JOURNAL

Do you have someone in your life who's just as focused and driven as you are? How have you been motivated by their ambition?

Are there others you've been waiting on instead of moving forward on your own path? How have they slowed down your progress?

Ask God to bring people who can help you maximize your potential.

How do you bring out the best in the people in your life?

PRAYER

God, thank You for the times of isolation. These times alone have helped me to realize the hunger inside of me. I pray that when the time is right You will bring into my life people who understand that I am destiny-focused. I'm thankful for Your perfect timing in my life, and for the people You place in my life according to Your infinite wisdom. Amen.

DAY 23

SET YOUR STANDARDS

We all must set our price, and it can't fluctuate depending on who's interested. Your price is your price. Those who want to be in your life can afford to invest or they can't.

Then Boaz told him, "Of course, your purchase of the land from Naomi also requires that you marry Ruth, the Moabite widow. That way she can have children who will carry on her husband's name and keep the land in the family."

RUTH 4:5 NLT

*O*ne of my favorite parts of vacationing at the beach is shopping. I don't mean going to a mall, either. I mean sitting on golden sands haggling underneath the warm sun. From sunglasses to home decor, almost everything comes along if you stay in one spot. What makes it the most fun is talking someone out of their price.

I've noticed these tropical entrepreneurs always manage to bring the price down once you seem to lose interest. Desperate for the sale, they start throwing in things for free or slashing the price in half. At the end of the day, my family and friends all gather for dinner and talk about the deals we made while relaxing on the beach.

Sometimes we conduct our relationships as if we are selling souvenirs on the seashore. Why do we insist on giving ourselves away? Offering up piece after piece of ourselves so that someone gets us at a steal? I don't know about you, but I want to be valued. If you don't see yourself as a gift, then who will? We must set our standards.

From the very beginning of their meeting, Boaz informed his kinsman of the terms. Along with Ruth, he would be responsible for having a child—heirs were vital to the family lineage—and caring for Naomi. These are the expectations that come with the responsibility. There was no sticker shock for Boaz; he knew the price and was gladly willing to pay it.

What are your expectations, your standards? In other words, what's your price?

Have you shared those expectations with others? We get upset when people do not live up to the standards we set, but often we have not even given them the courtesy of letting them know these standards exist.

Likewise, we cannot get caught up trying to meet the standards of others and fail to birth the vision God has for us. I'm here to let you know that God has placed talents and gifts inside of us—and He has plans for us to make the best use of those talents and gifts. Our faith teaches us that taking a stand to reach our goals may have a cost. People laughed at Noah and looked at David in shock. Those called by God must be willing to have faith strong enough to withstand the rejection of others around them.

There are some things in life that should be nonnegotiable. Your character, your self-esteem, your ambition are the things that make you, *you*! If someone wants to be in your life, you owe it to them to let them know up front what you will and will not compromise on. We all must set our price, and it can't fluctuate depending on who's interested. Your price is your price. Those who want to be in your life can afford to rise to the occasion. Don't give yourself away to the lowest bidder because you're afraid no one else will want you.

JOURNAL

List five nonnegotiable standards you have for your relationships.

Why are they so important to you?

Have you lived up to the same standards in return consistently, never ceasing? Have you been forgiving when others fall short?

Have you prayed over your standards?

PRAYER

God, help me to become a better version of me. I no longer want to bend my standards to accommodate another's insecurity. Lord, help me to walk boldly and proudly into my next level. As You develop me into a better person, I pray You will help me to eliminate anything that removes the ultimate standard: Your promise on my life. Amen.

DAY 24

BE HONEST

So often we take on person after person, struggle after struggle,
only to find ourselves completely depleted. We must know our
limits if we are to remain on the path to our divine destiny.

The closest relative said, "I cannot redeem it for myself,
because I would jeopardize my own inheritance. Redeem it
for yourself; you may have my right of redemption, for I cannot redeem it."

RUTH 4:6 NASB

I used to envy those people who could say no. It's not that I couldn't say it, but I didn't like to hurt people's feelings. It seemed like the more I didn't want to do something, the worse it became. I felt bad about agreeing to do something I didn't want to do, and even worse about not being able to say no.

Then I became one of those people.

I started to reason with myself. Is it better to disappoint someone up front or to start something knowing that I can't give 100 percent? I battled with this for so long before I realized that at the end of the day, I was doing them, and myself, a major disservice. I was spreading myself too thin trying to be what everyone needed me to be. Finally, I decided to be everything I want to be.

How often do we allow our hearts to commit to something we physically, emotionally, or mentally can't continue? So often we take on person after person, struggle after struggle, only to find ourselves completely depleted and unable to follow through. So often we see people who stop what they're doing to start something else. They become a jack- or jill-of-all-trades and master of none.

When Boaz approached the other kinsman, certainly this man had heard of Ruth. He undoubtedly knew her story and the tales that were told of her loyalty. Yet this kinsman still decided his inheritance was more important than the opportunity.

I have met countless people whom I feel I could be great friends with, but I really don't have time to invest in every one of these opportunities. It doesn't make the people bad or unworthy. It simply means I have to save a piece of myself, for myself, as well as for the others to whom I've already committed.

We don't have to create some huge profound reason for why we can't do something. We can simply say no and have peace about it.

For this other kinsman, it was as simple as, "I'm pursuing my inheritance and can't be distracted." He knew that if he married a Moabite woman, he would jeopardize his family inheritance. His decision cannot be deemed as either right or wrong but simply what was best for him at that time. Ultimately, the kinsman did everyone a favor. By being honest, he did not hinder Boaz or Ruth—or himself—from receiving God's best for their lives.

As you continue on your journey, you do not have to be connected with everyone you encounter. There are many people who will never be tied to your destiny, no more than this kinsman was tied to Ruth's. Be realistic about what you can and cannot handle. Do not let the fear of disappointing someone cause you to disturb God's master plan. Once you determine your purpose, stick to it and don't let anything distract you from staying the course.

JOURNAL

Do you ever worry about letting people down?

Are you losing yourself trying to help or befriend others?

How can you begin to eliminate the responsibilities and relationships that are weighing you down?

Each little piece of you counts. Make a list and prioritize what is most important in your life.

PRAYER

God, help me to be honest about my limitations. Help me to realize when some need me but when others need You. I don't want to be so wrapped up helping others that I cease to pursue my destiny. I pray that You give others the help they need to find their peace. Please give me the wisdom not to let people interrupt my peace or rob me of my ambition. Amen.

It's Already Done

When you are walking in obedience,
you have to believe God is going to cover you.

Now in those days it was the custom in Israel for anyone transferring a right of purchase to remove his sandal and hand it to the other party. This publicly validated the transaction. So the other family redeemer drew off his sandal as he said to Boaz, "You buy the land."

RUTH 4:7–8 NLT

$\mathcal{S}$omewhere on the other side of town, Ruth and Naomi were waiting anxiously to hear which kinsman redeemer would take Ruth as his wife. They had no clue that they were anxious for no reason. Long before Ruth met Boaz or even her first husband, Mahlon, God had predestined her steps. She was on reserve for her divine destiny.

How befitting it is that the kinsman takes off his shoe and gives it to Boaz. In their time, removing a sandal and handing it over was to say, "My feet will not walk on your ground." With this simple act, Ruth had officially become Boaz's betrothed, even if she wasn't aware of it yet. She may have felt nervous but had nothing to worry about.

Can you relate? Anyone who's been through what you've been through would have lost his or her mind by now. One thing after another, tears after tears, yet you are still here. Could it be that God has you on reserve? You may not realize it, but you were bought with a cost. You have been placed on reserve for a higher purpose.

That's why that accident couldn't kill you or the disease missed you. Through breakups and makeups, you were placed on reserve.

Ruth's situation reminds me of another passage that should give us confidence. Theologians believe that Genesis 3:15 is a prophecy of the coming of Christ: "And I will put enmity between you and the woman, and between your seed and her Seed; he shall bruise your head, and you shall bruise His heel" (NKJV). Here, after all that business with forbidden fruit, God tells Satan that the woman's offspring, humans, will always war against him. In fact, God promises that Eve's descendants will wound Satan's head, while he will only wound their heels.

It seems a bit unfair. A head wound is almost always more dangerous than a wound to the heel. Unless, of course, that heel wound makes you take a few missteps. When our heels have been bruised, we start to walk on land that we shouldn't. We begin to be poisoned by our own fear, bitterness, anger, and doubt. We cannot let what happened to us then consume us now.

Through Christ we are able to recover from the bruises of life that can lead us astray. Certainly Ruth knew all too well about the detours of life. As she waited for new information on where her journey would lead her, she had no idea God had already marked her path.

We often worry ourselves sick about something God has already figured out. When you are walking in obedience, you have to believe God is going to cover you. Whether things go the way you think they should or not, when you're walking with Him, you can trust that He will transform every trial.

Don't be tricked into thinking that just because you're delayed you're also denied. Stay the course, heal your heel, regain your footing, and prepare to use your destiny to wound the enemy's head.

JOURNAL

In what areas of your life are you waiting on God to move?

Have you committed those areas to prayer, or have you given up?

How can you exercise more faith and effort in the pursuit of your purpose?

What will you do once you've received your breakthrough? How will your life be different as you collide with your destiny?

PRAYER

God, I ask that You give me the patience to deal with silence. Help me to see that my faith must be proven, tested, and then stretched. I know that being a Christian is more than just quoting Scriptures and going to church. I believe in Your Word and trust that everything will work out for me. Even when You are silent, I trust that You still hear my prayers and see my faith. Amen.

"I Know You, and
I Still Chose You"

We often allow the things that almost broke us to define us and
keep us from reaching the next level.

Then Boaz announced to the elders and all the people, "Today you are witnesses that I have bought from Naomi all the property of Elimelek, Kilion and Mahlon. I have also acquired Ruth the Moabite, Mahlon's widow, as my wife, in order to maintain the name of the dead with his property, so that his name will not disappear from among his family or from his hometown. Today you are witnesses!"

RUTH 4:9-10

hen my sister and I were growing up, we fell in love with the movie *Pretty Woman*. It's the story of a young woman, living a less than desirable lifestyle, and a wealthy man who offers to pay her to accompany him to high-society events. In one scene, Vivian, the lead character played by Julia Roberts, walks into a fancy store on Rodeo Drive and is rudely ignored.

It's not that the sales staff don't see her; they just don't like what they see. She is underdressed and doesn't appear to have the income necessary to shop at their store. They were right about her and wrong about her at the same time. They could not distinguish her current state from the promise residing in her future.

She returns to the hotel embarrassed and upset because they confirmed what she has felt all along: She's not good enough. Later in the movie, after she has been expensively clothed and elegantly groomed, she returns to the same store. Instantly a snobby associate rushes to greet her. But Vivian reminds the snooty clerk of her previous visit and how she was treated. With her hands full of bags from the surrounding high-end boutiques, she tells the sales lady, "Big mistake! *Huge!*"

It's one of the most memorable moments in the movie. The core of what most people love about this part is the lesson it teaches. It's what anyone who has ever been labeled and misjudged desires others to realize. We should never judge someone before his or her transformation is complete.

Ruth probably knew what this feeling was like. The town's most respected man has declared his desire to marry Ruth to anyone who would listen. Ruth, the same foreign woman locals once whispered about, would soon be married to the esteemed and wealthy Boaz. Had they judged her when she was on the road to Bethlehem, they also would have made a "Big mistake! Huge!"

Too often we prefer to believe the things that almost broke us will keep us from reaching the next level. Clinging to such a false belief in turn relieves us of the responsibility of persevering. We think if we define ourselves by the past, then we don't have to try moving into the future. *Wrong.* Just because you once made poor decisions doesn't mean you can't be used for a better purpose.

God knows exactly who you are and the pain you've had to experience to birth your destiny. He knows everything, the good and the bad. He knows you and He still chose you.

JOURNAL

What's a remaining limitation on your journey to greatness?

Is it possible to use this to help you instead of letting it hold you back?

Can your story help someone else close a chapter in their life?

Name three things pain has taught you that might also serve as clues to your purpose.

PRAYER

Lord, I need Your help to forgive myself. I need to rediscover my worth. Help me to see that in spite of what I have felt, I still have purpose. Release me from the shame of my past. I want to be free from the memories that haunt me so I can walk boldly on the path before me. Amen.

DAY 27

WITNESS
THE REDEMPTION

You don't have to prove yourself to those who doubt you. When
you play your part and stay the course, God will vindicate you.

All the people who were in the court, and the elders, said,
"We are witnesses. May the Lord make the woman who is
coming into your home like Rachel and Leah, both of whom
built the house of Israel; and may you achieve wealth in
Ephrathah and become famous in Bethlehem. Moreover, may
your house be like the house of Perez whom Tamar bore to
Judah, through the offspring which the Lord will give you by
this young woman."

RUTH 4:11–12 NASB

The first time I went to see a professional basketball game, it was the Dallas Mavericks against the Los Angeles Lakers. Growing up, I had a very small, minor-stalker obsession with Kobe Bryant, but we'll save those stories for another time. So for my first game, I donned my Bryant jersey and walked proudly into the American Airlines Arena with my family.

It was great—our seats were so close I could see sweat dripping off the players! As we enjoyed the intense game, I made small talk with fellow Lakers fans around me. We laughed and made playful banter with the Mavs fans throughout the evening.

After a hard-fought battle, the Lakers finally won the game. As we were walking out to the car, we ran into some members of our church. They had seen us during the game but couldn't get our attention. One of the deacons mentioned to me how cool it must have been to watch the Lakers game with the owner of the team. I looked over my shoulder, searching for whomever he was talking to. Then I realized he was talking to me!

I had no clue that I had been sitting beside Jerry Buss, the owner of the Lakers, the entire game. I certainly didn't ask, and he didn't mention it. We simply enjoyed watching the game together. He modeled a profound truth for me. When you are truly comfortable with who you are, you don't have to convince others of your worth.

In time, others may find out, maybe they won't, but neither should determine how you live your life.

Without trying to defend against every vicious attack or track down every person who ever said anything about her, Ruth gained the respect of everyone in Bethlehem when Boaz chose her. He stood with Ruth, and because of his position others saw her differently. Ruth didn't have to scheme for attention or revenge; she just had to go about the business of surviving.

Sometimes we're tempted to announce our redemption to validate our worth. But when you play your part and stay in position, God will vindicate you. The same mouths that once talked badly about you will be telling others they're proud of you. Be comfortable enough with who you are that you don't feel the urge to prove yourself to everyone you encounter.

There was no need for Mr. Buss to prove his worth to me at the Lakers game or for Ruth to prove her worth to the town. All she needed to do was live a life that would tell the story on its own. You don't have time to change the thoughts of everyone who ever believed differently about you. You don't have time to tell everyone your worth. Instead, let your worth do the talking.

JOURNAL

How have you handled rumors or gossip in your own life?

When you walk into a room, does your presence reflect your pain or your destiny?

You can't control what others think about you, but you do control what you project. What little changes can you begin to make that will allow others a preview of your healed future?

List those who have seen the wrong turns on your journey and yet still see your worth.

PRAYER

God, when You deliver me, help me to be humble enough to forgive. I want to release the anger I felt about the people who devalued me. I want to release the feelings of hurt from gossip. I know You have plans for me that are bigger and better than I can imagine. I just hope You will teach me the art of redemption. Amen.

FROM REDEMPTION TO RESTORATION

Restoration is one step beyond redemption. It is the moment when God shows you that you lost nothing in the process.

So Boaz took Ruth and she became his wife. When he made love to her, the Lord enabled her to conceive, and she gave birth to a son. The women said to Naomi: "Praise be to the Lord, who this day has not left you without a guardian-redeemer. May he become famous throughout Israel! He will renew your life and sustain you in your old age. For your daughter-in-law, who loves you and who is better to you than seven sons, has given him birth."

Then Naomi took the child in her arms and cared for him. The women living there said, "Naomi has a son!" And they named him Obed. He was the father of Jesse, the father of David.

RUTH 4:13–16

*T*here are moments during pregnancy, especially for first-time mothers, when you feel like you're losing more than you're gaining. During labor pains, you don't have a concrete understanding that the increasingly painful contractions will give way to this beautiful soul you will soon hold in your arms. It's not until that instant of finally holding your newborn that you know you would do it all again, all for that timeless moment in which you are forever changed.

Many women can give birth, but it takes a mother's heart to love a child. From the time that infant is placed in her arms, she silently vows to walk through life with him or her. Her sole mission is to be the child's protector. Without even having to think about it, a mother commits to seeing problems before they happen, handling each day with care, sheltering her child.

In the same way, God is not only our Creator but also our loving Father. He created us with a purpose and loves us too much to let us go. Even when we can't understand the painful losses in our journey, we have to realize that He is working out the details of our destiny.

Boaz helped deliver Ruth, but only God could restore her. Ruth had been content living in Moab as Mahlon's wife. But God led her and Naomi back to Bethlehem, where Boaz redeemed her from her past and then God restored all that she had lost. No longer would they face famine, for God had blessed them with one of the most abundant fields. No longer would Naomi know sadness, for God had given her a grandson to rejuvenate her joy. Ruth was no longer a widow, but rather the wife of a well-respected man. Naomi, who had lost two sons, now had the love of a daughter-in-law who had proven she was worth seven sons.

Restoration is one step past redemption. It is the moment when God shows you that you lost nothing in the process. All the tears you cried and pain you felt were a part of the plan. Anyone who has experienced the exceedingly abundant blessings of God knows that the pain pales in comparison to His restoration.

When you give your life to God, all the seeds you sow will reap a harvest you can't even imagine. Ruth was first married to a man who left his homeland because of a famine. She went back to his land and married Boaz, the owner of one of the largest fields. She never had children with Mahlon, but with Boaz she became a mother. Ruth certainly sowed many tears, but she reaped incredible joy.

Your story is not over yet. Don't harden your heart and block the seeds from being sown. Keep your heart open and available to God. The pain may be devastating. There will be days when you want to give in and give up. You'll want to numb the pain with a masquerade, but don't. Keep walking. Keep your heart alive. And one day you'll be like Ruth, blessed by the same things that once broke you.

JOURNAL

Ruth recovered more than she lost. But she had to have less than she hoped for first. In what areas have you experienced having less than you hope for?

Boaz told the whole community about his love for Ruth. How is God revealing your destiny to those around you?

Who are the people God has brought into your life to share your destiny?

If you want to sow healthy seeds with your abundant blessing, you have to be willing to stretch. Are you ready to lose your control over your life and receive God's direction?

PRAYER

Help me to deal with the pain of going to a new level. I want to use my blessings to help people, but I'm not sure if they'll accept me because of my past. All I desire is to help someone become free from the chains that once bound me. Give me the strength to go from redemption to restoration. Amen.

IT'S NOT ABOUT YOU

What if your struggles are not about you
but about the life that will be birthed through you?

Then Naomi took the child and laid him on her bosom, and became a nurse to him. Also the neighbor women gave him a name, saying, "There is a son born to Naomi." And they called his name Obed. He is the father of Jesse, the father of David.

Now this is the genealogy of Perez: Perez begot Hezron; Hezron begot Ram, and Ram begot Amminadab; Amminadab begot Nahshon, and Nahshon begot Salmon; Salmon begot Boaz, and Boaz begot Obed; Obed begot Jesse, and Jesse begot David.

RUTH 4:16-22 NKJV

*W*ho would've thought that a woman who started her life worshiping idols would be part of the ancestry of Christ? Ruth gave birth to Obed, who is the father of Jesse, who is the father of David. One simple act of not falling back into the Moabite mind-set after the death of Mahlon allowed her to become part of the lineage of Jesus Christ.

You may think that your survival is just for you, and that's why it's easy to let life beat you down. But it's more than that.

Christ faced His own obstacles and struggles on the road of His divinity. But He would survive and go on to fulfill His destiny, just like those who came before Him. Your commitment to surviving leaves an inheritance to your family. Only those who care to study Ruth's life understand the trouble she faced on the road to her destiny. Her story reminds us that it's not all about us. We think our survival is just for us and that's why it's tempting to stay down when we fall.

So often we remember Ruth with Boaz and her ultimate blessing, not with her struggle. This outcome gives me comfort. It means when all is said and done, my legacy will not be *what* broke me but *how* God blessed me. Only those who care to see my scars will understand that the blessing did not come without wounds and that I did all I could to survive.

So what story will your wounds tell? Will they be of the bitter infection you let seep into your heart? When a wound is infected, it doesn't just affect the open area; it spreads and hurts other areas of the body. Suddenly, your whole body is trying to compensate for this one hurt area.

Don't wear your heart down trying to overcompensate for the area where you lost pieces of yourself. Instead, confront the pain. Try again. Someone is watching who will need to be reminded that you made it and they can too.

We never know who will be affected by our survival. In the moment, it's hard to see outside of the pain. Only when you dare try to heal will you discover the purpose for your pain.

And, yes, you will have to dare. It may feel uncomfortable at first. You may have to stretch out of your comfort zone. But your blessing is worth the risk. It's worth the pains that come with growth.

Now, more than ever, we have to be brave enough to blaze a trail for one another. May our lives be an example of grace. Remove the facade and admit you're not okay, but you're working to get better. Believe that because of your decision to press forward, future generations will be able to do the same. I know this because Ruth, a woman with a painful past, gave us all a chance for a fruitful future.

JOURNAL

If your story ends before the healing, what will the world know about you?

How has your pain hurt the people around you? How has God used it to bless them?

What lesson did you learn through your pain that you hope teaches generations to come?

If your pain saves just one person, it will have served a greater purpose. How can you use your painful past to bless others with a fruitful future?

PRAYER

Lord, in the moment, the pain hurts so much I can't imagine how it could help someone else. I just need the strength to endure so that I can tell others about Your grace. I want to turn my wounds into wonders and my pain into purpose. The only way the darkest days of my life can transform into light for someone else is if I realize it's not about me. It's about You! Amen.

COLLIDE WITH
YOUR DESTINY

You may have to face the pain of crashing, deal with the
memories of what happened, and confront the anxiety of what
led you to that moment. You may even be worn down to pieces.
But it may be the only way you can collide into your destiny.

"Praise be to the Lord, who this day has not left you without a
guardian-redeemer."

RUTH 4:14

ecently in Bedford, Virginia, an SUV crashed, causing six passengers to be thrown from the vehicle. The injuries sustained were so extensive that one of the adults and a small child had to be airlifted. The other survivors from the accident were taken by ambulance to the nearest trauma center. All but one were accounted for. A small infant, just a few weeks old, could not be found.

The survivors knew it was unlikely the baby survived. If the impact of the accident didn't kill him, then being thrown out of the vehicle so violently probably did. When the fire department arrived at the scene to determine the quickest way to clean up the debris from the accident, they were also hoping to find the remains of the infant and give the family closure.

What they found stunned everyone. As they lifted the remaining wreckage, they heard the cries of a baby. Trapped under the hood of the large SUV was the car seat the infant had been strapped into at the beginning of the journey. Still secured into the car seat, frightened but unharmed, was the baby they never thought could have survived. From all accounts he should have been dead, permanently injured, or drastically scarred.

Yet somehow the baby was spared.

If someone examined your life and wrote all the details of your collision on paper, others might think your chances of survival were slim to none. Yet here you are. God has spared you and placed your life on reserve.

Your collision was never intended to kill you, so do not let it. Long before your journey began, God strapped you in and promised to protect you from even the most horrific of tragedies. Perhaps at times you stopped trusting Him to see you through and allowed fear to unharness the hold He has on your life. Yet you are still here, and this is proof that He has not given up on you. So you cannot give up on Him.

We've all had our fair share of collisions. There have been moments when it seemed unlikely that we would survive, yet here we are. We may be bruised, but we will keep fighting. We may get burned, but we won't be consumed. We may be afraid, but we won't stop living.

We don't know why we've had to face so many battles and obstacles in life. There is no true rhyme or reason to why someone like Ruth can be enjoying her life one minute, burying her husband the next, and then leaving her home for a strange land after that. At the time, it must've felt like she was taking one step forward and two steps back. The truth is, she was being pushed out so she could collide head on with destiny. Her plan for her life was good, but God's plan was great.

We have to give up our own desires in order to seek the will of God. When our own plans fail, we cannot become bitter and decide to let go. God is constantly protecting us, even when we face the most awful collisions. Like a small baby unlikely to survive a tragedy, we can make it beyond the pain and arrive at our ultimate purpose.

As broken as we may be, God wants to know we will give Him our all and allow Him to turn our lives into a masterpiece. Countless times Ruth had the opportunity to let the ghost of her past haunt the decisions of her present. We do, too. But I don't want to be controlled by my broken heart or my fear of history repeating itself.

When Ruth's story begins, we see her and Naomi at one of the darkest stages of their lives. When the story ends, their future seems filled with hope, prosperity, and joy. It doesn't mean that future is worry free and without obstacles. It definitely doesn't mean they have arrived at their destination. But they have realized their divine destiny and embraced it. Their story serves as a reminder that it's not about how you start; it's about how you finish.

Who could have guessed that the two broken women we met at the beginning of the story would each find her way back to joy. Different pasts yet similar hurts.

My story may be different from Ruth's, and yours may be different from Naomi's, but neither of our stories has to end where the hurt began. Refuse to bury yourself while there is still air in your lungs. Believe that God is capable of changing your life.

Sometimes the only way to fix a vehicle after an accident is to total it out and get a new one. Even with a new car, you can't change the way you received it. You can't separate the pain from the victory. If you're going to chase after God's best for your life, you must be willing to let your plans be totaled. You may have to face the pain of crashing, deal with the memories of what happened, and confront the anxiety of what led you to that moment. You may even be worn down to pieces. But how else can you collide with your destiny?

The only true way to kill the bitterness of your past is to seek the sweetness of today. There is beauty in struggle. No more than a painter's talent can be judged before she is finished can God's work in our life be judged in the middle of struggle. Don't give up on God because you feel you've been forgotten. You may only see a messy work in progress, but He is creating a masterpiece.

JOURNAL

At what point during the book of Ruth did you realize she was going to learn to live again? What strikes you as the turning point for her collision with destiny?

Where can you see glimpses of your own struggle in her journey?

How did she show God that she could handle more?

How are you showing God that you're strong enough to push past the pain?

Help someone who has been or could be broken in the same way you have been—for example, volunteer at church, mentor others, open communication with family and friends.

Ruth's journey has inspired many, but no one was more inspired than Ruth herself. Do you have what it takes to live an inspired life? What will sustain you?

PRAYER

God, I know my life has had many detours. I know that many times I hoped things would go one way and they went another. I didn't mean to make my will more important than Yours. Somehow I just lost myself, trying to find myself. I need the courage to find myself again, but this time I want to find the person You created me to be. I tried it my way. I created an image of what happiness looked like and I lost it all. You are the only One capable of locating my broken pieces and making me whole again. Here I am, God; I need You like never before. Please open my heart so that I can feel, love, and trust again. I want to be the person I was created to be. Please take the wheel and guide me. I'm ready to collide with destiny. Amen.

SARAH JAKES is a businesswoman, writer, speaker, and media personality. She currently oversees the women's ministry at The Potter's House of Dallas, a multicultural, nondenominational church and humanitarian organization led by her parents, Bishop T. D. Jakes and Mrs. Serita Jakes. In addition to her duties at The Potter's House, Sarah periodically serves as host of *The Potter's Touch*, a daily inspirational broadcast airing on several national television networks.

Prior to joining the staff at The Potter's House, Sarah worked with TDJ Enterprises, where she was responsible for grass-roots marketing efforts for the feature film *Not Easily Broken.*

After graduating from high school at the age of sixteen in the top 10 of her class and in the top 10 percent of the nation, Sarah attended Texas Christian University, where she studied journalism. She regularly blogs at sarahjakes.com on love, life, family, and marriage and aspires to write articles and books that chronicle the lives of young women who have overcome extreme challenges to reach their goals in life.

When she is not pursuing her career endeavors, Sarah enjoys cooking, listening to music, and spending quality time with her two children.

Many assume that a pastor's kid should have life figured out, should have it all together. Imagine instead being fourteen, pregnant, and the daughter of a megachurch pastor ... and a divorcée by age twenty-five. Sarah Jakes has overcome much in her life, and now has a heart for women whose lives have had unplanned detours, either due to their own mistakes or some other loss or heartache. Both a memoir and a book that inspires, *Lost and Found* shows women how God can and does work all things together for their good.

Sarah's unfailingly honest account of her journey will inspire and encourage women of all ages. Her readers will understand that if God can take a lost, confused teen and heal her, He will do the same for them.

" I don't remember a time where I didn't have my son. From the moment I held him in my arms, it was like everything that happened before him was lost in the hopes of his future. By the time I reach the age of twenty-nine, I will have spent more of my life as a mother than not. And while I wish that I could've honored the beauty that is in his soul with a more traditional entrance into the world, the truth is—he saved me. Saved me from things I am yet discerning. My greatest fear was how people would judge me, judge him, or use statistics to predict our future. I was ashamed for him, for me, for my parents and their work, for my siblings, and for my friends. I carried the weight of my choices with me. With this albatross around my neck, I was determined to live a life of atonement to those who had been affected by what I had done. I wanted to clean up the mess I had made in the best way possible. I wanted to put a Band-Aid over a gunshot wound. In time I would learn that until I confronted my desire to seek the approval of others, I would never fully embrace me. "